FOUR PLACES

FOUR PLACES

≒A PLAY≓

JOEL DRAKE JOHNSON

NORTHWESTERN UNIVERSITY PRESS

EVANSTON, ILLINOIS

Northwestern University Press
www.nupress.northwestern.edu

Printed in the United States of America

10 9 8 7 6 5 4 3 2 1

LIBRARY OF CONGRESS
CATALOGING-IN-PUBLICATION DATA

Johnson, Joel Drake.
    Four places : a play / Joel Drake Johnson.
        p. cm.
    ISBN 978-0-8101-2574-2 (pbk. : alk. paper)
    1. Family—Drama. I. Title.
PS3610.O3566F68 2009
812.6—dc22
                            2008048242

In memory of Jane Salzmann, and
Raymond and Henrietta (Burwell) Johnson

For Larry B. Salzmann

CONTENTS

ACKNOWLEDGMENTS

The author wishes to thank Mary Ann Thebus and Sandy Shinner, whose work as actor and director inspired him as he wrote the play. He also wishes to thank Edward Sobel and Dennis Zacek for their professional encouragement; and Kerry Maguire, James Horwath, J. Stephen Richards, Carlo Franco, and Randy Orians for their stories and observations.

PRODUCTION HISTORY

Four Places received its world premiere at Victory Gardens Theater (artistic director, Dennis Zacek; managing director, Marcie McVay) in Chicago, Illinois, on March 28, 2008. It was directed by Sandy Shinner, Victory Gardens' associate artistic director. Designers for *Four Places* were Jack Magaw (set), Carol J. Blanchard (costumes), Avraham Mor (lights), and Andre Pluess (sound). Tina M. Jach was the production stage manager. The cast was as follows:

Peter Burns . . . . Warren
Meg Thalken . . . . Ellen
Mary Ann Thebus . . . . Peggy
Jennifer Avery . . . . Barb

Four Places was a finalist for the National Arts Club Best Play of 2006 and was nominated by the Joseph Jefferson Committee for Best New Work (2008).

FOUR PLACES

CHARACTERS (in order of appearance)

Warren, middle-aged man and Ellen's younger brother

Ellen, middle-aged woman

Peggy, the mother of Ellen and Warren

Barb, a waitress, about the same age as Ellen and Warren

[*The setting is a small city just outside of Chicago in the present. The play takes place in four different playing areas, all of which should be suggested by action and minimal setting and furniture and should appear separate: a car, the foyer of a restaurant, a table or booth in the restaurant, and a women's bathroom represented by a stall.* PEGGY's *house is offstage. The stage direction "Drive" is something akin to a silence that measures the discomfort of the characters; "Beat" is a very short pause. We should be able to see the characters move from one area to the other. In the first scene,* ELLEN *is in the driver's seat of a car.* WARREN *sits next to her. There is a brief pause. They look at one another.*]

WARREN: Well . . .

ELLEN: You want me to go in?

WARREN: How do you usually—

ELLEN: I usually walk her out.

WARREN: No, I'll—

ELLEN: She's at the door.

WARREN [*looking*]: She is?

ELLEN: I just saw her look out the window. She's trying to figure out who you are. She's wondering why I'm not getting out of the car. She's wondering if something is wrong, some problem.

WARREN: OK—

ELLEN: I always walk her from the house.

WARREN: All right.

[WARREN *opens the car door.*]

Fuck, I don't know.

ELLEN: What?

WARREN: Fuck.

ELLEN: Well, we have to do something, don't we?

WARREN: Yes.

ELLEN: Jesus, look.

[WARREN *looks toward the house.*]

WARREN [*chuckling*]: She's crazy. What's she doing?

ELLEN [*also chuckling*]: I see her.

WARREN: What is that? It's like some kind of dumb show—what is she doing?

[WARREN *chuckles.*]

Jesus. Shit. Fuck, fuck.

[*Opening the car door*] Fuck. OK!

[WARREN *is gone.* ELLEN *turns on the CD player and listens intently to a Mozart piano sonata, but without any visible reaction. This goes on for a bit. She looks off. She turns off the music as we see* WARREN *and* PEGGY *approaching the car.*]

PEGGY: What a surprise. Ellen didn't tell me you were coming. You're the reason we're late!

WARREN: There's no school today—

PEGGY: What?

WARREN: Ride up front.

PEGGY: I don't mind the back.

WARREN: Ride up front, Mom.

[WARREN *opens the car door.*]

PEGGY: ELLEN:
You've got those long legs.   Get in back, Mom.

WARREN: I don't have long legs. When I was ten, I think I had long legs. Now they're just legs. And they bend.

PEGGY [*chuckling to herself*]: They bend. I know they bend.

[PEGGY *gets in the front seat.* WARREN *shuts the door and gets in back. They mime putting on seat belts as* ELLEN *pulls away. They drive for a bit.*]

ELLEN: Those were funny faces you made.

PEGGY: What funny faces?

ELLEN: Looking out the window.

PEGGY: Did you see those?

[*Drive.*]

I didn't think you saw those.

ELLEN: Right.

PEGGY: I didn't.

[*Drive.*]

Did you notice what the neighbor did?

ELLEN: I saw.

PEGGY: All those bushes. Pulled them out. And they came close to getting the mock orange but I went out and I told them, "That's my mock orange." You remember the mock orange, Warren?

WARREN: What?

PEGGY: The mock orange. You trimmed it every year.

WARREN: I hated the mock orange. You should have let them cut it down.

PEGGY [*to* ELLEN]: I made him trim that bush every year.

WARREN [*as* PEGGY *chuckles*]: What?

PEGGY: He'd shoot me these dirty looks—

WARREN: What?

PEGGY [*continuing*]: —the entire time. Are you all right in the back?

WARREN: I'm fine. Very comfortable.

[*Drive.*]

PEGGY: Your car still smells like new.

ELLEN: I've had it a year.

PEGGY: It smells like new.

WARREN: I hate that mock orange.

[*Drive.*]

ELLEN: Look at that girl, Mom.

PEGGY: Oh, my god, I can see her crack!

WARREN: What?

PEGGY [*loudly*]: I can see that girl's crack! Oh my god! That's not one of your students, is it, Warren?

WARREN: No.

PEGGY: If it was, I'd say she needs to stay after school.

[*Beat.*]

But not with Warren.

[PEGGY *and* ELLEN *are chuckling.*]

WARREN: What?

[*Drive.*]

Not much traffic.

PEGGY: No.

[*Drive.*]

WARREN: Did you see what they did to the post office?

ELLEN: It looks stupid.

PEGGY: Where are we looking at?

ELLEN: The new sculpture.

PEGGY: Oh.

ELLEN: It's moronic. It's cheap.

WARREN: It is cheap.

PEGGY: What is it?

WARREN: It's called *On Earth as It Is in Heaven.*

PEGGY: Oh. I like it.

ELLEN: Oh, Mom, it's terrible. It makes us look moronic.

[*Drive.*]

PEGGY: I guess it's religious then . . . Amen.

ELLEN: What?

PEGGY: Amen.

[*Drive.*]

    I hadn't seen it.

WARREN: Just went up.

[*Drive.*]

PEGGY [*referring to a new place*]: I wonder how they're doing?

WARREN: OK, I think.

ELLEN: I like it there.

WARREN: Never been.

ELLEN: It's not bad.

PEGGY: Jackie told me it gave her indigestion.

ELLEN: Did she?

PEGGY: She's never going back. Have you seen her? She's gained so much weight. My god. I don't know how she gets around. I worry for her, pulling all that weight around.

[*Drive.*]

Oh, ah, Paul Pierce died.

ELLEN: Really?

WARREN: Who?

ELLEN AND PEGGY: Paul Pierce.

WARREN: He died?

PEGGY: He was sixty-eight and had cancer.

WARREN: Boy, that's young.

PEGGY: I'll say it's young.

WARREN: What kind of cancer?

PEGGY: Esophagus.

WARREN: Did he smoke?

PEGGY: He smoked. They found it and then a month later he was dead.

WARREN: Really?

PEGGY: Thirty days. That's what I want; I want them to find it and then give me a month to make my arrangements.

[*Drive.*]

Don't hook me up to anything.

[*Drive.*]

Or I'll come back to haunt you.

ELLEN: We won't.

PEGGY: Warren?

[*Drive.*]

Warren?

ELLEN: Warren—

WARREN: What?

ELLEN: Mom's talking to you.

WARREN: What?

PEGGY: Never mind.

WARREN: What did you want?

PEGGY: I don't want to be hooked up.

WARREN: To what? What are you talking about?

ELLEN:	PEGGY:
Never mind. It's called life support.	To one of those life pipes, whatever you call them. The name escapes me.

[*Drive.*]

WARREN: I don't either.

[*Drive.*]

ELLEN: I saw him, you know, just a couple of weeks ago. He was speaking through a kind of tube speaker in his throat—

PEGGY: Did you say hi?

ELLEN: I did.

PEGGY: Did he know you?

ELLEN: I doubt it.

PEGGY: They say it's one of the worst kind of cancers.

ELLEN: Why do they say that?

PEGGY: I don't know. It's painful, I guess.

ELLEN: Some cancers are painless?

PEGGY: I don't know, I just read that it's one of the worst.

[*Drive.*]

I don't know if Patty is working out.

ELLEN: Why is that?

PEGGY: She bought me this family-sized container of ketchup.

ELLEN: So?

PEGGY: I don't want a large container of ketchup. I want a small container.

ELLEN: Did you tell her?

PEGGY: I told her, but she told me she was saving me money. And I said, "Well, Patty, how much did you save me?" and she said she figured I saved twenty cents and so I just laughed and I said,

"Patty, just buy me the small ketchup. I can handle a smaller container better than the large, and so I would prefer the small." You know what she did?

ELLEN: What?

PEGGY: She started to cry.

ELLEN: Why would she cry?

PEGGY: I think she might be just a little bit unstable. Not a lot, just a little. You know, her sister is a schizophrenic.

ELLEN: I didn't know.

PEGGY: She lived in a halfway house for years—until she woke up one night and burned the place down.

ELLEN: Oh, come on.

PEGGY: It's what I heard. Five people died. Now she's in prison. It's a sad thing, but insanity runs in the family, in the genes, unavoidably Darwinian, and I think you and—

PEGGY [*not stopping*]:
—your brother need to know that. You should also know that she was very keyed up today.

WARREN [*on "know that"*]: What was that?

WARREN: Who are you talking about?

ELLEN: Patty.

WARREN: What happened?

ELLEN: Mom made her cry.

PEGGY: I didn't make her cry. She's a schizophrenic. She has no control of her emotions.

WARREN: What did you do, Mom?

PEGGY: I told her I preferred small containers to large containers. That's all that I said. That's it.

ELLEN: She tries too hard.

PEGGY: I think she tries too hard.

[*Drive.*]

But I like her. She's very nice. For a schizophrenic.

[*Drive.*]

She gets bossy, but I don't mind much.

ELLEN: You call me when she starts chasing you with a knife.

PEGGY [*chuckling*]: Oh, OK. I'll do that. "Help, help, she's chasing me with a knife!"

ELLEN [*playing along*]: Let me load the dishwasher and I'll be right over.

[*They both chuckle. Beat.*]

PEGGY: And why are you here today, Warren? I know you said—

WARREN: What?

ELLEN: He has the day off.

WARREN: What?

ELLEN: You need a hearing aid, Warren.

WARREN: I can't hear.

ELLEN:	PEGGY:
Yes, we know.	We know that. Why do you have the day off?

WARREN: There's no school.

PEGGY: Why is there no school?

WARREN: It's a holiday.

PEGGY: What's the holiday?

WARREN: It's just a school holiday.

PEGGY: Oh. What is that?

WARREN: Just a holiday for students and teachers. An institute.

PEGGY: Oh.

WARREN: We do this occasionally.

PEGGY: Oh. A holiday for students and teachers. I've never heard of it. Does it have a name?

WARREN: What's that?

PEGGY: This holiday you and the students are on.

WARREN: It's just an institute.

PEGGY: Institute day.

WARREN: That's right.

[*Drive.*]

PEGGY: Well, it's nice to have you along.

WARREN [*bringing his hand up to touch her shoulder*]: Nice to be along.

[*Drive.*]

PEGGY: I was surprised when you came to the door.

WARREN: That's what I wanted. I wanted you to be surprised.

PEGGY: And you got what you wanted.

[*Drive.*]

    I hope it's not busy.

ELLEN: It never is.

PEGGY: Well, with school off and everything.

ELLEN: It'll be fine.

[*Drive.*]

PEGGY: Warren?

WARREN: What?

PEGGY: Never mind.

WARREN: What?

PEGGY: Nothing. I won't say it.

WARREN: OK.

[*Drive.*]

PEGGY [*to* ELLEN]: I think Warren's skipping school.

[*Drive.*]

    [*To* ELLEN] Don't you think?

ELLEN: I don't know.

[*Drive.*]

PEGGY: I think there's something up, isn't there?

PEGGY:	ELLEN:
Warren?	Like what?

WARREN: What? I can't hear—

PEGGY: So is there something?

ELLEN:	WARREN:
No.	It's a lunch.

PEGGY: Oh.

[*Drive.*]

Then it should be fun.

[*Drive.*]

ELLEN: I'm going to let you two out.

PEGGY: I can walk.

ELLEN: You can get a table.

[*She pulls over.* PEGGY *and* WARREN *start to get out of the car.*]

PEGGY: Thank you.

WARREN: Any place special?

PEGGY:	ELLEN:
We have our usual.	Some place in the back.

PEGGY: Or in the back.

WARREN [*he opens* PEGGY's *door*]: You got it there?

PEGGY: I'm fine. You don't want our usual, Ellen?

ELLEN: Let's try the back.

PEGGY: The back's OK.

[PEGGY *and* WARREN *walk into the restaurant.* PEGGY *sits on a bench as* WARREN *looks for the hostess.* ELLEN *parks the car. Once she does, she turns on her Mozart piano sonata and listens for a bit as* PEGGY *and* WARREN *talk in the foyer of the restaurant.*]

WARREN [*returning*]: Five minutes.

PEGGY: Five minutes. Usually we get right in.

WARREN: Not today.

PEGGY: I guess twenty minutes makes a difference.

[*Silence.*]

We're usually here a little earlier.

[*Beat.*]

That's your fault, you know.

WARREN: Sorry.

PEGGY: I'm just kidding.

WARREN: I know. So what are you going to have?

PEGGY: My usual.

WARREN: What is that?

PEGGY: Caesar salad with salmon bits.

WARREN: Sounds good.

PEGGY: It's pretty good. It's good. They dip the salmon into a light coating of flour. It's their secret. Shhh.

[*Silence.*]

Ellen has never been happy.

WARREN: Why do you say that?

PEGGY: Because she has never been happy. She seems to have a secret life going on inside of her—

WARREN: We all have secret lives inside of us—

PEGGY: I don't.

WARREN: You do.

PEGGY: I tell you I don't. I'm right here. Here I am.

WARREN [*shaking her hand*]: Pleased to meet you.

PEGGY: What's your secret life?

WARREN: It's a secret.

PEGGY: You should tell your mother everything.

WARREN: You should tell your mother nothing.

PEGGY: I might be able to help you out.

WARREN: I don't need it. I love my secret life!

PEGGY: We all need help figuring things out.

WARREN: Do we?

PEGGY: Yes. At some time. Some, all the time. Everyone else, sometimes.

WARREN: I'm OK.

PEGGY: I think something is going on. What is it, Warren?

WARREN: Nothing.

PEGGY [*putting her head in her hands*]: Ahhh, no. That's worse. You saying that—

WARREN: Nothing is going on.

PEGGY: So much worse.

WARREN: We will talk about it at lunch.

PEGGY: Does Ellen have cancer?

WARREN: What?

PEGGY: She's always been so unhappy—no kids—

WARREN: No.

PEGGY: —and I've always thought she would die before me.

WARREN: No, Mom.

PEGGY: Since Richard passed—

WARREN: Ellen is tough—

PEGGY: But she worshipped him—

WARREN: She loved him: he was her husband—

PEGGY: He never liked me.

WARREN: He liked you.

PEGGY: And I tried, but he would never talk to me.

WARREN: He was a quiet man. An artist. Artists are quiet people.

PEGGY: Are they?

WARREN: And, anyway, what's not to like?

PEGGY: That's what I thought. He would talk to your dad, but he was distant with me. After all those years, still distant. And then he gets sick and he dies and I just thought—well, I worried that she might—I don't know what I thought—she should have never gone to Italy—

WARREN: It was OK.

PEGGY: She got depressed—

WARREN: I don't think she did—

PEGGY: She could have gotten sick—

WARREN:	PEGGY [*not stopping*]:
She's fine.	—with the bird flu.

WARREN:	PEGGY:
She's not sick.	It's all over Italy.

WARREN: She's not.

PEGGY: Good.

[*Silence.*]

WARREN: And I'm fine, too.

PEGGY: I wasn't worried about you.

WARREN: Thanks.

PEGGY: You've always been very consistent in your moods.

WARREN: You should see me in my secret life.

PEGGY: Tell me.

WARREN: I am very moody. Violent mood swings.

PEGGY: Well, keep it to yourself, then.

[*They share a chuckle.*]

You see Catherine?

WARREN: No! Why would I see Catherine?

PEGGY: You were married to her.

WARREN: Not anymore.

PEGGY: You should be friends.

WARREN: No, we shouldn't. Why would you say that? Why would you think that? You act like you don't know anything about the situation.

PEGGY: I just think people should try to forgive.

WARREN: Forget, maybe.

PEGGY: Well—

WARREN: Drop it, please, Mom?

PEGGY: I like her.

WARREN: I hate her. Drop it.

PEGGY: I hope you don't talk to your students like this.

WARREN: I do, sometimes. If they deserve it.

PEGGY: Well, I just think it's sad—

[ELLEN *comes in.*]

ELLEN: We're waiting?

PEGGY: Five minutes.

WARREN: It's a little busy.

PEGGY: We're not our usual time, Ellen. And that's Warren's fault.

WARREN: Sorry.

PEGGY: I'm teasing—

ELLEN: I'm surprised. It's never busy.

PEGGY: We are not our usual time. Oh, here she comes.

BARB [*entering*]: You're back!

PEGGY [*standing to greet her*]: How are you doing?

BARB: My favorite girl. I was looking for you.

PEGGY: We brought the boy so we're a little late. This is my son, Warren.

BARB: I've heard about you. And you're nothing like your mother described.

WARREN AND PEGGY [*as* BARB *laughs*]: What?

BARB: I'm kidding! You should see your faces! We love your mother; she's our favorite customer.

WARREN: And she's our favorite mother.

PEGGY: Warren is a—

PEGGY AND BARB: —teacher.

BARB: I remember; you told me. I was a terrible student. You wouldn't want me in your class. I was mean, I was mouthy—can't believe that, can you?

WARREN: Well—

BARB: I hated school. So you playing hooky?

WARREN: School holiday.

BARB: I dropped my kid off today. You're playing hooky. I don't mind.

PEGGY: I don't understand.

BARB: Oops. I'll write the note!

ELLEN: I'm ready to sit.

BARB: And how are you?

ELLEN: I'm fine, thanks. In the back somewhere, Barb.

BARB: This way then.

PEGGY [as BARB leads them]: Is there school today?

BARB [to ELLEN]: So you haven't been around.

PEGGY: Ellen has been in Italy.

BARB: Italy.

PEGGY: Two weeks. She didn't like it.

ELLEN: I liked it.

BARB: Homesick?

PEGGY: She could've gotten sick. Everybody over there is dying of the bird flu! She's lucky she didn't wind up in an Italian hospital. We're going way back there?

BARB: The request was made—

ELLEN: That's fine, Mom. Let's just sit.

PEGGY: But I can't see anyone from back there. I like to see people and I can't see anyone—

ELLEN: You'll have a full house view.

BARB: I like this table myself. What do you think, Warren?

WARREN: Fine with me.

BARB: You gonna be OK with this, sweetie?

PEGGY: It's fine, I guess. Whatever the kids want, I guess.

BARB [*pulling out a chair*]:   WARREN [*pulling out a chair*]:
You want to sit here?   How about here?

PEGGY: Either one is fine. I'll sit here. Where are you sitting, Ellen? There?

ELLEN: Right here.

[PEGGY *looks at* BARB.]

BARB: That's fine with me. I'm just offering, that's all.

[*As everyone takes a seat,* BARB *hands out menus.*]

    I want everyone to be comfortable. A couple of specials, just so you know. The soup is a potato leek. We got a special entrée; it's a pork tenderloin and it is delicious; I've been snacking in back. And the fish today is an orange roughy served with broccoli.

PEGGY: Anything we shouldn't have?

BARB: The roughy is rough. A little tough. But it's generally a kind of tough fish so it depends on your taste. OK? A minute to think it over? I know you always get the salmon Caesar—

PEGGY: And my rum with Diet Coke.

BARB: I saw Magee making your drink when you walked by.

PEGGY: Was he?

BARB: He was.

PEGGY: He's a sweet man.

[PEGGY *looks over and waves at the bartender.*]

And nice looking, too.

BARB: You are too much. You guys better watch her. She'll be going home with the bartender.

PEGGY: Ohhh.

BARB [to WARREN]: And how about you, teach?

WARREN: I need a minute.

BARB: You got a minute. Ellen, same for you, do you think?

ELLEN: A minute.

BARB: Water OK for everybody?

WARREN:	ELLEN:	PEGGY:
Just water, yes.	Yes, thank you.	I don't want any water.

BARB: I know that! OK, I'll be back.

[BARB *leaves. Long pause.* PEGGY *is looking around.*]

PEGGY: I don't see anyone I know.

WARREN: Who are you looking for?

PEGGY: People that I know. Do you see anyone?

ELLEN [*looking around*]: No.

PEGGY: That's a pretty sweater, Ellen.

ELLEN: You've seen this. I got it in Italy.

PEGGY: No, I haven't. Let me touch it.

[ELLEN *holds her arm out.*]

ELLEN: It's cashmere.

WARREN: How was the trip?

ELLEN: OK.

PEGGY: That's a good color for you. [*To* WARREN] She got lonely.

ELLEN: I did not get lonely. I met people there.

PEGGY: You said you were lonely.

ELLEN: I was a little lonely. But I liked the sights. I liked the ruins.

PEGGY: The ruins are nice.

ELLEN: The Vatican was creepy—

PEGGY: We talked about this. I loved the Vatican.

ELLEN: It's a creepy, scary place. Deeply, deeply morbid.

PEGGY: Well, I was overwhelmed by it.

ELLEN: Exactly. Warren, you walk into St. Peter's Square and that awful fascist architecture looms over you and surrounds you like a marbled mausoleum—

PEGGY: I found them lovely.

ELLEN: —trapping you inside; the ghost of popes past intimidating you—

PEGGY: The ghosts of what?

ELLEN [*not stopping*]: —into doing their bidding, which is to fear God, give ten percent or more of your earnings to old men who can then luxuriate—

PEGGY: Ohhh.

ELLEN [*not stopping*]: —in a palace slash mausoleum with large beds, silk sheets, and altar boys.

PEGGY: Well, I was a twenty-year-old virgin who was thinking of being a nun. I guess it felt a little different.

ELLEN: Mom.

WARREN: What did she say?

PEGGY [*loudly*]: I was a twenty-year-old virgin! [*In a regular voice and chuckling at her joke*] I think you just don't listen, Warren. I think you're tuning us out.

WARREN: I hear you.

BARB [*entering*]: Got your rum and Coke, sweetheart, right here.

PEGGY: ELLEN [*chuckling*]:
Thank you.   I wasn't crazy about it.

BARB: WARREN:
Magee's got another one waiting   Obviously.
in the wings so you holler—

PEGGY: I will.

BARB [*as she sets down water*]: We all ready to order?

PEGGY: Well, you know what I want.

BARB: And I got that here, sweetie.

ELLEN: Orange roughy for me.

BARB: It's a little tough now.

ELLEN: I like a tough fish, thank you.

WARREN: Potato-leek soup. The large size.

BARB: That's it?

WARREN: On a diet.

PEGGY: That's all you want, Warren?

WARREN: I'm not hungry. And I'm trying to lose a little weight.

BARB: So I'll bring you a little bread.

WARREN: That's fine.

BARB: You don't look fat.

WARREN: Thank you.

BARB: I'll have that order up in a minute.

PEGGY: Tell Magee the drink is perfect. [*To the bartender, mouthing the words in a harsh whisper*] Thank you. It's delicious.

BARB [*as she goes off*]: I'll let him know.

PEGGY: She gets a little familiar, I think. You know who she is, don't you?

ELLEN: I know.

PEGGY: I know you know.

WARREN: Who is she?

ELLEN: Vi Hanson's daughter.

WARREN: Don't know him.

ELLEN: Vi is a woman's name, Warren.

WARREN: I've never known anyone named Vi.

PEGGY: Of course you have.

WARREN: Who?

ELLEN AND PEGGY: Vi Hanson.

WARREN: That was a little loud.

ELLEN: She was Dad's secretary at the store. She fell in love with Dad.

WARREN: I didn't know this.

ELLEN: I can't believe you didn't know—

PEGGY: Ellen was always spying on your dad and me.

ELLEN: I wasn't.

PEGGY: You'd listen in on our conversation then come up to me later and ask me about it. [*To* WARREN] You were always hiding under the table with your head in a book.

ELLEN: So her husband came to the house—

WARREN: What?

ELLEN: We were both at home with Mom; Dad was at work and this—

PEGGY: Howard.

ELLEN: Howard Hanson comes to the house to tell Mom—

PEGGY: He wanted to warn me—

ELLEN: That his wife was in love with Dad.

WARREN: Are you kidding me?

PEGGY: I told Howard—I called him Howie—that I was glad he told me and we'd just have to wait to see how things played out. That night I talked to your dad and told him—

ELLEN: That he'd have to fire her or he'd have to quit his job.

PEGGY: Well, she quit. That's what happened.

WARREN: See, I didn't know.

ELLEN: Head in a book.

PEGGY [*giggling at times during these lines*]: I prayed so hard that night. I thought maybe he loved her, too. That happens all the time and so I prayed and I sprinkled some holy water I got when I visited Italy, you know, when I was a student, bought a whole gallon. I sprinkled some in your dad's coffee the next morning and, lo and behold, it worked.

[WARREN *and* ELLEN *laugh.*]

I sprinkled some, too, when you were trying out for that play in high school and wanted to be in it so badly and you got the part!

ELLEN: You thought you had talent.

PEGGY: And I used it on you, too, Ellen, but it didn't work.

ELLEN: Oh.

WARREN: What?

PEGGY: Let's just say it didn't work.

ELLEN: OK.

PEGGY [*whispering as she refers to* BARB]: I doubt that she knows.

ELLEN: Oh, I don't know about that.

PEGGY: I don't think so. In fact, I'd bet on it. She looks just like her mother.

[PEGGY *takes a drink.*]

So . . . What is this all about?

ELLEN: What?

PEGGY: You two. I know something is going on. What is going on?

ELLEN: Let's wait until we eat.

WARREN: I thought we were—

PEGGY: I can talk and I can eat at the same time. So what is going on? Are you moving, Ellen?

ELLEN: No.

PEGGY: Warren?

ELLEN: No, he's not moving.

PEGGY: And I know that you're not dying—

ELLEN: Dying?

WARREN: It's about you and Dad.

PEGGY: What about us?

ELLEN: The living situation.

PEGGY: We do fine. Patty comes in a few hours a day—that's something that could be changed—

ELLEN: She says Dad is always drunk on the couch, that you feed him watered-down scotch all day.

PEGGY: Patty's a liar.

WARREN: She seemed pretty certain, Mom.

PEGGY: And you told me this was a school holiday so—

WARREN: I'm sorry—

PEGGY: What was that about, lying to your mother?

WARREN: A white lie.

PEGGY: Oh, so we're coloring our lies? If that's what we're doing, I'm going to start telling blue lies—

WARREN: OK, Mom—

PEGGY: I don't like your tone. It's a red tone, I think.

WARREN: Stop doing that—

PEGGY [chuckling]: Well, so who am I supposed to trust here? Patty buys containers that are too large—

ELLEN: She is telling us—

PEGGY [*softly*]: A white lie.

ELLEN [*not stopping*]: —that you give Dad drinks all day.

ELLEN:	PEGGY:
All day, Mom.	Not all day.

PEGGY: And so what? I've always done that. It's his only happiness—

WARREN: The problem, Mom, is that we had talked about that—

PEGGY: But it was impossible to stop—

WARREN: Maybe it would help—

ELLEN: Do you sit down with him?

PEGGY: Do I sit down with him? I don't get what you mean.

ELLEN: Are you drinking with him, Mom?

PEGGY: I have a drink, yes; I have a drink, I drink with him, I mix it, I mix two drinks, and I sit with him.

WARREN: It might help if you didn't—

PEGGY: And who are you? Who are you to tell me that, Warren? With your problem.

ELLEN: Mom—

PEGGY: He has a problem. Let's talk about his first.

WARREN: I've worked things out—

ELLEN [*to* WARREN]:	PEGGY:
She knows you have. Mom?	I'm doing the same thing. I'm working on my problems.

PEGGY: I just don't know what the two of you think you're doing unless it's attacking me. Is this some kind of planned raid, some kind of planned attack on me—I feel like Iraq. I feel like Iran!

BARB [*coming to the table*]: Lunch is served.

PEGGY: My kids are attacking me, Barb. Can you save me?

BARB [*as she serves*]: What are they doing?

PEGGY: Attacking me. From all sides.

BARB: You all aren't attacking my favorite customer, are you?

WARREN: No.

BARB: This is the sweetest woman I've ever known.

ELLEN: Sweeter than your mother?

BARB: Sweeter than my mother.

PEGGY: Thank you.

BARB [*still serving*]: There's your soup and bread. You sure that's all you want?

WARREN: Yes.

BARB: How's that fish, that orange roughy, look to you, Ellen?

ELLEN: It looks good.

BARB [*to* PEGGY, *who holds up her glass*]: I know what you want. Coming right up.

[BARB *exits. There is a long pause. They look at their food.* PEGGY *is the first to take a bite. Then* WARREN. *Then* ELLEN. *A few moments of very tense silence as they eat.*]

PEGGY: Bet that fish is tough.

ELLEN: It's fine.

WARREN: We love you, Mom.

[PEGGY *smiles at him.*]

ELLEN: We love you and Dad.

[PEGGY *smiles and eats.*]

We have great respect for what you two did for us.

PEGGY: What did we do?

WARREN: A lot.

PEGGY [*taking a pen from* WARREN'*s shirt pocket*]: Here. Make a list. Start your list. What did we do?

ELLEN: We're not making a list—

WARREN: You raised us, you loved us, you gave us food and shelter, you sent us to school, you paid our way through college. Ellen went to Dartmouth, which was very expensive—

PEGGY: Yes. Took all our savings—

WARREN: —you taught us the value of life, to save our money, to be kind to others—

ELLEN: Wash the dishes and clean our rooms—

PEGGY [*eating still*]: What about our living condition? We provided a nice house. [*Chuckling a bit*] See, I can eat. I can talk, too.

[BARB *comes back.*]

BARB: Here's your drink, sweetie. They being nice?

PEGGY: They're trying.

WARREN: We're trying.

BARB: Cut off your legs if you're not.

[BARB *laughs.*]

Enjoy your lunch.

[BARB *exits.*]

PEGGY: Go ahead.

ELLEN: Patty has said things—

PEGGY: She's an idiot. A schizophrenic—

ELLEN: Stop doing that.

PEGGY: She comes from a long line of crazy people. What has she said?

ELLEN: That you broke a set of dishes—

PEGGY: I dropped them.

ELLEN: She said it looked like you had thrown them on the floor of the basement—

PEGGY: Well, that's not accurate—

WARREN: From the top of the stairs.

PEGGY: I dropped them.

WARREN: She said it looked like you had thrown them.

PEGGY: Well, looks are deceiving, aren't they?

WARREN: She said—

PEGGY: I don't care, Warren. And if I did throw them—

ELLEN: Did you throw them?

PEGGY: I got mad and I threw them. I'm sorry. It won't happen again. Done. [*Chuckling*] Drinking gin makes me angry. Rum keeps me sweet.

[PEGGY *chuckles again. She sips her drink. She begins to eat. There is a pause as they all begin to eat.*]

ELLEN [*calmly*]: There are things she says you're saying to Dad. Things you are doing to Dad.

PEGGY: And you believe her? She's a stranger in our house. What do you even know about her?

WARREN: We just want to ask you about some of the things she has said—

PEGGY: And you'll believe me?

WARREN: Yes.

PEGGY: And you?

ELLEN: Yes, we'll believe you.

PEGGY [*still casually eating*]: So what did that nutty girl say?

ELLEN: She heard you say mean things to Dad.

PEGGY: Mean things? What is that?

ELLEN: You call him names.

PEGGY: I've always called him names. What names?

ELLEN: You know what names.

PEGGY: I don't. I don't call him names. Never. Ever. Done.

WARREN: Mom—

PEGGY: You said you would believe me. You said that.

ELLEN: Do you threaten him?

[PEGGY *stops eating. Pause. She starts to get up.*]

PEGGY [*calmly*]: I have to go to the bathroom, that's all.

ELLEN: OK.

PEGGY: I'll take my purse.

ELLEN: You want me to go with you?

PEGGY: Would you go with me?

ELLEN: If you want me to.

PEGGY: I would like you to go with me.

[ELLEN *and* PEGGY *both go.* WARREN *looks around. He begins sipping his soup. He stops and just sits there as the lights come on in the bathroom, where* ELLEN *stands outside the stall. Beat.*]

    Ellen.

ELLEN: I'm here.

PEGGY: Would you come in?

ELLEN: You want me to come in?

PEGGY: I would like you to come in.

[ELLEN *goes in. She closes the door behind her so we can only hear their voices.*]

    What is that?

ELLEN: You're bleeding.

PEGGY: You think that's blood?

ELLEN: Yes, I think it's blood.

PEGGY: Well, I've been bleeding for about two weeks now.

ELLEN: Two weeks?

PEGGY: What does that mean?

ELLEN: It means you should have said something much earlier.

PEGGY: You think it could be serious?

ELLEN: It could be serious.

PEGGY: Oh.

[*Silence. The toilet flushes. They come out.* PEGGY *washes her hands.*]

ELLEN: I'll take you to the doctor tomorrow if you want.

PEGGY: I don't want.

ELLEN: Well, you should see someone.

PEGGY: I should?

ELLEN: Yes, you should.

PEGGY: OK. [*Very gently taking* ELLEN *by the arm*] What is going on? What is the plan here?

ELLEN: We are here to talk about the plan.

PEGGY: And do I get a say?

ELLEN: Let's go talk to Warren.

PEGGY: Is he running the show? Is he the boss, Ellen?

ELLEN: Everything will be all right.

PEGGY [*putting her head in her hands*]: Oh, no.

ELLEN: Mom—

PEGGY: I am going to have no say—

ELLEN: We are talking about it, Mom. Warren and I—

PEGGY: Takes the both of you? Why does it take the both of you? Why are you surrounding me, Ellen?

ELLEN: We don't mean to surround you.

PEGGY: But I feel completely surrounded. This is supposed to be our lunch. Not Warren's. He should be in school. He shouldn't be here.

ELLEN: Warren—we don't mean to make you uncomfortable.

PEGGY: You don't mean to—

ELLEN: Come out and talk to the both of us.

[PEGGY *puts her head in her hands. Beat.*]

Mom.

[PEGGY *keeps her head in her hands.*]

Let's see if we can't make a plan. Make a decision.

PEGGY: But why today? Why on our lunch day? This is my favorite day of the week.

ELLEN: Patty called this morning and told us—

PEGGY: She's unstable; she's bossy and mean—and you listen to her? As if the world wasn't ruled by enough crazy people. Lunatics in the street, roaming the highways, now in my house? [*Suddenly leaving*] Thank you for looking at my urine.

[PEGGY *leaves, then* ELLEN. *They return to the table.*]

WARREN: Everything OK?

PEGGY: I have blood in my urine. I wanted to show Ellen.

WARREN: What?

ELLEN: It looks like blood in her urine.

PEGGY: I was worried and I wanted to show Ellen, but other than that . . .

[*Silence.* PEGGY *begins to eat again and drink—so does* ELLEN *and then* WARREN.]

WARREN [*breaking the silence*]: So what would that mean?

PEGGY: I don't know.

ELLEN: I bet you're dehydrated. That drink will dehydrate you.

PEGGY: Well, then, I guess I'll drink some water.

ELLEN: You need to see a doctor, but I wouldn't—

WARREN [*handing her his glass of water*]: Drink more water, will you, Mom?

PEGGY [*as she takes the water*]: I just thought you should know.

[*Silence. They eat a bit.*]

I told him if he didn't stop his complaining I would leave him. I said I would throw him out. I say that all the time; I have said that exact same thing since we got married; you've both heard me say it a million times. And that's all.

WARREN: That's all?

PEGGY: Yes.

WARREN: Patty said you threatened to kill him.

[*Everyone stops eating.*]

She heard you, she says.

PEGGY: She hears voices—

WARREN [*pushing*]: She says she's heard you say it more than once.

PEGGY: She has a hearing problem. [*Chuckling*] She's like you. She can't hear a thing.

WARREN: She said you were practically killing him with a pillow—

PEGGY: Did she? When? When did she see me do that?

WARREN: Early this morning. She came in. She came in early she said because she had a lot to do around the house—

PEGGY: She does nothing really.

WARREN: You stopped when she walked in. She said you were both— she said you were both—she said you were both drunk.

PEGGY: I was not drunk this morning.

WARREN: Drunk, she said. And you were kind of lying all over him—

PEGGY: Oh, for heaven's sake—you shouldn't be talking about that sort of thing—

WARREN: —and had a pillow over his head and that you were forcing the pillow, she thought over his head, so that he would suffocate.

PEGGY: I don't know why she is saying that. I don't understand why she dislikes me so much; I am very nice to her.

WARREN: Why—

PEGGY: I don't know why, Warren. How would I know why? How can you expect me to know why? I haven't known why for a very long time. I used to think I knew why about a lot of things, but not anymore. I have to go to the bathroom again, Ellen.

WARREN: You just got back.

PEGGY: I think I need to go again. I am positive. Can I go, Warren, to the bathroom? I have blood in my urine.

WARREN: Mom.

PEGGY [*to* ELLEN]: Will you go with me?

WARREN: Mom—

PEGGY: I know when I have to go and when I don't have to go and right now I have to go.

ELLEN [*as* PEGGY *leaves*]: I'll catch up. [*To* WARREN] Fuck.

WARREN: What?

ELLEN: Fuck, Warren.

WARREN: What? What should I do?

ELLEN: I don't know, but somehow—

WARREN: I don't know what to do; I don't how to do this. Tell me.

ELLEN: I don't know, Warren.

[ELLEN *hurries off.* BARB *enters.*]

BARB: Everything OK?

WARREN: Yes, thank you.

BARB: She's not in trouble, is she?

WARREN: No.

BARB: I can go help if there's anything.

WARREN: Thank you. Ellen's with her.

BARB [*as she takes* PEGGY's *glass*]: I can freshen this up.

WARREN: That's all right.

BARB: I should probably freshen—

WARREN: That's OK.

BARB: She's hardly touched it.

WARREN: Just bring a glass of water.

BARB: She usually has three.

WARREN: She doesn't need it. She's fine.

BARB: Oh, but I know what she wants.

WARREN: Don't bring her another drink.

BARB: But it's all watered down now . . . You let me know, teacher.

WARREN: I will.

[BARB *leaves as lights come up on the bathroom.* PEGGY *is in the stall.* ELLEN *stands outside.*]

ELLEN: What's happening, Mom?

PEGGY: Not much, really.

[PEGGY *sighs rather loudly.*]

ELLEN: OK?

[PEGGY *sighs rather loudly again.*]

   You OK?

PEGGY: Your father fell in love with Vi. He told me.

ELLEN: Oh.

PEGGY: Did you know?

ELLEN: I didn't . . . I did . . . I did know . . . He told me, too . . .

PEGGY: Oh.

[PEGGY *sighs deeply.*]

ELLEN: I asked him.

PEGGY: Oh.

ELLEN: And then I told him that he should tell you.

[PEGGY *sighs deeply.*]

PEGGY: Well, I guess I don't have to go.

[PEGGY *flushes the toilet and comes out.*]

You must have been—

ELLEN [*holding up ten fingers*]: Ten.

[PEGGY *washes her hands. She finishes.*]

PEGGY: I like to come here and look at Barb. I like to come here and talk to Barb and have her fawn all over me. I don't know why.

ELLEN: She's very nice to you; she's very attentive.

PEGGY: I am hoping that it's only dehydration.

ELLEN: I think that's probably all that it is.

PEGGY: What other things are there?

ELLEN: I don't know.

PEGGY: You're a doctor.

ELLEN: A psychologist.

PEGGY: But you don't know?

ELLEN: I wouldn't wager a guess except to say that lots of people get infections—

PEGGY: So that's probably what it is.

ELLEN: Probably.

PEGGY: I still love you, by the way.

[*Beat.*]

I do. I still love you.

[PEGGY *and* ELLEN *exit to the table.* WARREN *still sits, looking straight out.*]

WARREN: Are you all right?

PEGGY: It was a false alarm.

ELLEN: She's all right.

PEGGY: I bet everyone's lunch is cold. Is your fish cold?

ELLEN: Yes, but it's all right.

PEGGY: Maybe we should pay the check and leave.

WARREN: I'm still eating.

PEGGY: Maybe you can get Barb to take it back and warm it up. Would you like her to do that, Ellen?

ELLEN: I'm fine.

[*Everyone begins to eat in silence.*]

WARREN: Mom.

PEGGY: I wasn't drunk this morning, but I had had a drink, but I had only one drink and I wasn't drunk. I got mad at your dad. I didn't really try to smother him. I didn't. But can I say something?

WARREN: Yes.

ELLEN: Of course you can.

WARREN: We want to hear your side of things.

PEGGY: Your dad and I actually have a life outside of yours. We have a relationship that is not part, any part, of who you are. We have our own little universe into which *no* one else is invited. A secret life—

WARREN: You told me you didn't have a secret life.

PEGGY: A white lie.

WARREN: So?

PEGGY: So some things, some things, Warren, are strictly *our* business. It's strictly us.

WARREN: What are you saying?

PEGGY: If we decide, then we decide.

[PEGGY *eats.* ELLEN *and* WARREN *look at her.*]

Do you remember how you would ask me not to trap the green mice?

WARREN: No, but I've heard the story—

PEGGY: I would set traps in the basement—that was when our house was actually on the outskirts of town, and we had mice from the field.

WARREN: I don't want—

ELLEN: Let her tell the story.

PEGGY: Thank you.

WARREN: But I—

ELLEN: It's not going to hurt you, is it?

WARREN: I've heard it. I don't remember it.

PEGGY: I was setting out traps for the mice, and you came down the stairs and you said to me: "Mom, please don't trap the green mice."

[PEGGY *chuckles a bit.*]

You didn't want me to kill any green mice.

[PEGGY *chuckles.*]

And so I didn't.

WARREN: I don't remember that story, Mom, but I do remember running around the house closing all the windows because you and Dad were yelling.

PEGGY: That happened once.

WARREN: Once during the summer. A couple of times during the winter. A few times in the spring and the fall.

PEGGY: Why are you so angry with me?

WARREN: Are you hurting Dad?

ELLEN: He's worried.

PEGGY: He's angry. Do you talk to your students like this? Did you talk to Catherine like this?

[*Quiet. They eat very small bits. This should be a breather for all of them.*]

ELLEN: So, Mom, have you tried to kill Dad?

[*Beat.*]

Have you tried to kill him?

PEGGY [*very softly*]: No.

WARREN: What?

PEGGY [*very softly*]: I don't use that word.

WARREN: What?

ELLEN [*overlapping*]: She said—

PEGGY: That is not the word—

WARREN: What is the word?

PEGGY: A white-lie word, I guess. So I guess, yes, sort of.

WARREN: Sort of?

PEGGY: I guess. I don't know. I guess I sort of have. I don't know—

WARREN: Mom—

PEGGY: Isn't this supposed to be a lunch?

ELLEN: What does "sort of" mean?

PEGGY:
Here we are at lunch and nobody is eating. I was hungry. If you had wanted to talk we could have talked at home. Why the concern? What is the sudden concern?

WARREN [*softly*]:
Can you tell us what you mean? Mom? Mom?

ELLEN [*overlapping*]:
We are concerned—

PEGGY [*very softly*]: Are you mad at me?

WARREN: What?

ELLEN: Have you tried to kill Dad?

[*A long pause as* PEGGY *eats a bit of her salad.* WARREN *starts to talk, but* ELLEN *stops him.* PEGGY *takes a piece of lettuce from her mouth. She puts it in a napkin. She looks at her children. She smiles weakly.*]

PEGGY: A little. He asks me to. And then sometimes, yes, sometimes I want to, but when I try to, I lose the strength one needs to kill someone. I lose it. I can't struggle enough. I can't focus enough and so it doesn't happen. But he has been asking me to, because, you know, he has such pain; he lies on the couch and can barely move and he stares straight up at the ceiling and he sometimes just shouts out, and what am I supposed to do? I can help a little. I can get him up enough to pee. I can bring him a drink of gin and set it by the table. But I don't know what else to do. And I would do what he asks, I would kill him, but I don't have the strength of his convictions.

[PEGGY *chuckles.*]

I don't have his strength. [*Very softly*] So there's nothing to worry about. I can't actually do it. I can't push myself that far. Are you mad at me?

WARREN: Yes!

ELLEN: Mom, we trust you—

PEGGY [*picking up her glass, putting it in the air, and rattling it*]: Barb, honey! [*To* ELLEN *and* WARREN] This is strictly between me and your dad.

WARREN [*as* BARB *comes on with a glass of water*]: You can't really say that, Mom.

PEGGY: Can I have just one more?

BARB:	WARREN:	ELLEN:
You sure can.	Mom, no more.	I don't think—

PEGGY [*to* BARB]: Can I have just one more?

BARB: You sure can. Anybody else?

ELLEN: No, thank you.

BARB: How about a drink for the schoolteacher?

WARREN [*shaking his head*]: No.

BARB: You know, I was just thinking—

WARREN: What's that?

BARB: I heard you weren't teaching anymore.

WARREN: What?

ELLEN: He's teaching—

BARB: I must have misunderstood.

WARREN: I still teach at the high school.

BARB: I thought I'd heard.

ELLEN: You must have misheard.

BARB: How about a glass of wine, Ellen?

ELLEN: No—

PEGGY: She's got piano practice.

BARB: Ohhh. Yeah, I guess I misheard.

PEGGY [*taking charge*]: And I think we are all about done here so you want to take our dishes and bring us a dessert menu?

BARB: You've hardly touched your meals.

PEGGY: I think we're done.

WARREN: Fine.

BARB: Waste of food—you want me to wrap this?

PEGGY: Not for me.

WARREN: No.

ELLEN: I'm still working.

BARB [*starting to take* ELLEN's *plate and then putting it back*]: Oh. I'll take these—

PEGGY: And dessert menus.

BARB: On my way.

[BARB *starts to exit.*]

PEGGY [*as* BARB *exits*]: Thank you . . . They have great desserts, Warren.

WARREN: OK.

PEGGY: You should try one.

WARREN: I'll probably pass on the desserts.

PEGGY: You should try one. Your day off of school. Your white-lie holiday. You should have a dessert.

WARREN: I don't want a dessert. I want to talk about—

PEGGY: Ellen, you want—

ELLEN: No. I still have my fish—

PEGGY: I was sorry you didn't like Italy.

ELLEN:	WARREN:
It was fine.	Stop doing that.

PEGGY: I can't imagine, though, going to Italy and thinking it was only fine.

WARREN: Stop.

PEGGY: What?

WARREN: We have to get through this.

PEGGY: We have to get through?

WARREN: Yes.

PEGGY: What? The end of my life? What did she mean, do you think? You don't teach—

WARREN: She's crazy.

ELLEN: Mom.

WARREN: I don't know.

ELLEN: You're changing the—

PEGGY: ELLEN:
He cries sometimes, I've told you: he cries   Mom.
sometimes. And now look at Warren; Warren,
please don't—

WARREN: Mom—

PEGGY: I threw the dishes down the basement stairs because he kept teasing me—

WARREN: I don't understand.

PEGGY: I told him that every time he yelled out her name, I was going to break a dish. And so he did and so did I. He kept yelling, "Vi Hanson." And I kept throwing plates and "Vi Hanson!" *Crash!* And "Vi Hanson!" *Crash.* Until I'd broken fifty-two dishes!

WARREN: Holy shit.

PEGGY: Please don't—I would like to have dessert; I would like to enjoy at least one part of this meal, but if you keep looking like that. Ohhhhhhh.

[PEGGY *drops her head into her hands. There is a silence again, a silence that lasts until* BARB *comes back with menus and a drink for* PEGGY.]

BARB [*to* PEGGY *as she sets down her drink*]: Are you all right?

PEGGY: I am all right.

ELLEN: She has an upset stomach.

BARB: You want me to get you something?

PEGGY: Do you have a gun? I'd like to shoot my children. Bang, bang. Two bullets, one gun served over brown rice.

BARB: Ho, ho, ho, ho. They're that bad?

PEGGY: Yes. They should be shot. They really should. That's how bad they've been.

BARB: You guys! What are you doing? So you still want that dessert?

PEGGY: Yes. Please. Do you two mind if I have dessert?

ELLEN:	WARREN:
Of course not.	No.

ELLEN: We don't need menus.

BARB: All right.

PEGGY:	BARB:
You know what I want.	But I know what you want!

BARB: I set one piece aside just for you.

PEGGY: They don't have my sweet tooth.

BARB: That's why they're not sweet, right?

PEGGY: Right!

BARB: One chocolate brownie–nut fudge bar à la mode—

BARB AND PEGGY: With the chocolate sauce.

[PEGGY *laughs.* BARB *starts to leave.*]

PEGGY [*after* BARB]: Oh, ahh, bring three forks!

BARB: I'll get that dessert.

ELLEN AND WARREN: Thank you.

[BARB *leaves.*]

PEGGY [*sipping on her drink*]: We'll have a nice dessert and then—
Warren, look at me. What have I done? Look at me, Warren.

ELLEN [*softly but very sternly*]: Look at Mom!

[WARREN *looks at* PEGGY.]

PEGGY: Don't you think there are some things that happen between two
people, between people who have been with one another for fifty
years or so that is completely private? That no one should know,
should have any information, some things so private, so unknown
about them, don't you think, don't you think? Would your dad
want you to know? Would your dad want you to say anything?

WARREN: At some point, Mom, we no longer have any rights. We've
given them up. At some point. If you try to kill someone—murder
my dad—

[*The following exchange between* PEGGY, WARREN, *and* ELLEN *is very
rapid.*]

PEGGY: You think that?

WARREN: Yes.

PEGGY: So easily you think that.

WARREN: What else—

PEGGY: You go there so quickly.

ELLEN: Warren doesn't know how to say things very well, does he?

WARREN [*softly*]: Fuck you, Ellen.

[PEGGY *puts her hands over her ears.*]

PEGGY: Don't.

WARREN:	ELLEN:
I'm trying very hard.	God, Warren.

WARREN:	ELLEN:
I am protecting Dad. We're protecting Dad. I love Dad, too, Mom.	Have some respect—show some respect—she is not a murderer.

WARREN: What do you call it, then?

ELLEN: Show just a little—

WARREN: I am.

ELLEN: Show more then.

PEGGY: You know, your father and I bought four plots in the cemetery in case one of you might need it. But I may sell it. How would that be, Warren?

WARREN: Mom.

PEGGY: I think the price of cemetery plots has gone up; you know, they've really done some beautiful landscaping—

WARREN: Do what you want, Mom. If you need the money—

PEGGY: That is not the point.

WARREN: I know it's not.

PEGGY: Should I sell your spot or not?

WARREN: I don't care. It's not important to me. Sell it!

ELLEN: Shut up, Warren.

[*Beat.*]

PEGGY [*calmly, even folding her napkin very carefully*]: Right before Patty came in this morning, your father and I were having gin, watered-down gin because he said he hurt, he was begging me for it, screaming my name. And so I got out of bed and made him a drink. I do that because it will calm him, because it helps him. And it was early, very early and still dark outside, and we were drinking watered-down gin and eating a few stale peanuts that were in a bowl on the coffee table within his reach, and at first we were talking sweetly, laughing a little bit even. And we were talking about the parties we would have and the people we would invite, and you two wanting to stay up late to participate, and how Ellen would cry when we would say no; we even sang a couple of songs by Perry Como and the Ray Charles Singers, you remember? And we started arguing about a few of the words we were singing from "Moon River" and he said those aren't the words—and I knew he was wrong because I was thinking straighter than he was, but he kept insisting that it was "wider than your smile."

[PEGGY *chuckles a bit and continues.*]

And I said, "No, it's 'wider than a mile.'" But he said there's no poetry in that. And I said, "Well, I think there *is* poetry in 'wider than a mile.' Poetry is in the details," I said. "Not the similes. Not the obvious metaphors." And he starts saying I was nuts and that it's too bad I wasn't as pretty as Audrey Hepburn and I told him she had anorexia so he must be attracted to stick figures and that just drove him crazy. And it got worst with him singing "wider than your ass" and "your face just like a bass"—and then calling me crazy and stupid and even saying I was a coward for staying with him all this time, and I said, "Don't you remember how we both sang 'Two drifters off to see the world'?" We sang that together. And he says, "If you have the nerve, if you have the guts, you'd take that pillow there and you would put it over my face," he said, "and you'd choke the breath right out of me." "Right out of me," he said. "I won't fight you," he said. And I was crying and he's yelling and saying stuff about Vi Hanson—how she looked like Audrey Hepburn, how he sang "Moon River" with her—and so I said, "All right, old man," and I took the pillow and put it on his face. But I can't press hard enough really; it was a joke, really, how ineffective I was, and so he tells me to lay on top of him, that my weight on top of him will make the difference, and so I do, I lay on top of him, and I press and shout out to him, "Is it working? Are you dying?" And he yells back, "Not yet, bitch!" And I press as much as I can and I say, "Are you dead yet?" and he says, "No, I'm still breathing." And he says, "You're pressing on my forehead not my nose and mouth; my nose and mouth are not on my forehead; you've got to press on my nose and my mouth, that's how I breathe," he says and we start to laugh. And I say: "I know how you breathe," and he says, "Come on, get it over with, please, Peggy! I'm in pain, I'm in pain, I'm in pain." And so I move it a little, the pillow, and he tries to grab me and push me into him. But you know, he's weak and skinned like a bone, and I'm saying, "Let me know when you pass," and I start singing "Moon River," but with the correct words and very softly like a dirge—and that's when the insanity-laden Patty comes breaking into our house. *If it is any of your business.*

[PEGGY *gets up.*]

I have to go to the bathroom.

WARREN: Again!

ELLEN: Let her go to the bathroom, Warren.

WARREN: But we're not done.

PEGGY: I have to go.

WARREN: We're not done.

PEGGY: Verdict's in. Guilty, guilty, and guilty. Convicted. Life. And, thankfully, I've served my sentence.

[PEGGY *starts to exit.*]

WARREN: Leave the drink, Mom.

PEGGY: What?

WARREN: The drink.

PEGGY: Oh.

[PEGGY *sets it down and leaves.*]

ELLEN: We'll tell her on the way home.

WARREN: Did you not just hear all that?

ELLEN: Yes.

WARREN: Jesus fucking Christ, what's been going on—

ELLEN: It's not me and it's not you.

WARREN: But how long do you think—

ELLEN: Why do you have to ask—

WARREN: Because we should have been doing something.

ELLEN: We're doing something—

WARREN: Jesus fucking Christ, why didn't we know about this?

ELLEN: Because we don't live our parents' lives.

WARREN: You see them more—

ELLEN: You blame this on me, are you kidding?

WARREN: But you're more in touch—

ELLEN: OK, that's it. We're going.

WARREN: We're not done—

ELLEN: We can tell her in the car—

WARREN: In the car?

ELLEN: I won't go through this with you—I won't go through this!

WARREN [*softly*]:
I'm sorry. I'm sorry. I'm sorry.
I'm sorry. I'm sorry. I should
have never said that.

ELLEN [*softly*]:
How dare you? How dare you?
Because I see Mom and Dad
more than you, this is my fault?

WARREN: No.

ELLEN: What?

WARREN: No. I'm sorry.

ELLEN: This is much more upsetting—

WARREN: You're the one who wanted to come here—

ELLEN: I thought being here would keep her from exploding, but
    you've been so hard on her—

WARREN: I am doing what I think—

ELLEN: And you're blaming me.

WARREN [*overlapping*]: I am not the bad guy. I did not try to suffocate my dad.

ELLEN: Neither did I . . . We can't stay here, Warren.

WARREN: But in the car? In the car?

ELLEN: We did this wrong.

WARREN: She'd tried to kill him—

ELLEN: You call Patty.

WARREN: We said an hour.

ELLEN: We're not going to make it—call Patty.

WARREN: All right!

ELLEN: There is something about this that just reeks of bad form, bad judgment.

WARREN: Are we supposed to let Mom murder—

ELLEN: That's not what it is.

WARREN: What is it then?

ELLEN: Don't call it that.

WARREN: Go check on her.

ELLEN: Don't ever call it that.

WARREN: You made me the heavy.

ELLEN: You played it.

WARREN: You forced it.

ELLEN: Nobody forced you.

WARREN: Go check on her.

ELLEN: Fucking jerk.

WARREN: Yeah. Whatever.

[ELLEN *leaves.* WARREN, *as his mother did, puts his head in his hands. Lights on in the bathroom.* PEGGY *stands in the middle of the bathroom as* ELLEN *enters.* PEGGY *and* ELLEN *face each other.*]

PEGGY [*smiling nicely*]: Funny meeting you here.

ELLEN: Do you have to go to the bathroom?

PEGGY: I wanted to know what was going to happen next. What's my punishment?

ELLEN: When you come out and we both can talk to you.

PEGGY: Boy, I just have no control here at all, do I?

[*Beat.*]

You know what I asked for when I sprinkled the holy water into your orange juice?

ELLEN: I don't want to know.

PEGGY: I asked that the Virgin Mary allow you to forget everything you'd overheard me—

ELLEN: Oh, Mom.

PEGGY [*not stopping*]: —and your dad say, because I thought it had made you so unhappy.

ELLEN: I am not unhappy.

PEGGY: And when it didn't work, when our lady didn't take away your memory, I realized that it must be easier to get someone a role in the high school play than it is to make them forget the words and the voices that made them unhappy.

ELLEN: I am not unhappy, Mom.

PEGGY: I know you miss Richard—

ELLEN: You don't know, Mom—

PEGGY: I would have sworn.

ELLEN: We've never talked about it.

PEGGY: But I've asked. I was always asking.

ELLEN: And we are still not talking about it.

PEGGY: But why?

ELLEN: Because I don't want to.

PEGGY: All right.

ELLEN: And I am not unhappy.

PEGGY [*going into the stall*]: If you say so. [*From the stall*] What is next?

[*Silence.*]

What is next?

[*Silence.*]

She doesn't answer. I should write your name and your number on this wall, Ellen, and tell people that if they want a good time they should call you.

[*We hear* PEGGY *laugh inside.* ELLEN *joins her.*]

I should write that, for good head, call Ellen.

[PEGGY *and* ELLEN *both laugh.*]

I'm not even sure what that is.

[PEGGY *and* ELLEN *are still laughing.*]

But I figure if you graduated from Dartmouth, you must have a good head so you can give it to someone else.

[PEGGY *laughs.*]

ELLEN: What are you doing, Mom?

PEGGY: I'm talking dirty.

ELLEN: You want to talk about blow jobs, Mom? You want to hear about the times I've given men blow jobs? I've got a long list of blow-job experiences—let's start with, oh, I don't know, how about—

PEGGY [*overlapping on "blow-job experiences"*]: No! No! No! No! No! No! No! No!

ELLEN: Then finish going to the bathroom, please.

PEGGY: Are you going to wait?

ELLEN: I don't have to.

PEGGY: I wish you would.

ELLEN: I'm waiting.

PEGGY: Well, I want you to wait. How are the piano lessons?

ELLEN: I love them.

PEGGY: You should come to the house and play for your dad. He always loved to hear you play the piano.

ELLEN: Your piano is out of tune.

PEGGY: I'll get it tuned tomorrow. How about that?

[*We hear* PEGGY *going to the bathroom.*]

Well, it's beet red. Did you want to see it?

ELLEN: No. It only takes a small drop—

[*The toilet flushes. Beat.*]

It only takes a small drop of blood to make it red.

PEGGY [*coming out of the bathroom*]: Is that true?

ELLEN: Yes.

PEGGY: And why is that?

ELLEN: Urine is almost colorless and so a little red—

PEGGY: Oh, god, what if I die before your dad? What then? What will happen?

ELLEN: Jesus, Mom—

PEGGY: You and Warren will have to—do you think Warren is unhappy?

ELLEN: No. Yes, yes, I think he's unhappy.

PEGGY: He is so mean today. I'm trying to figure that out. He has always favored your dad, but I don't understand this behavior. This is why Catherine left him, I bet.

ELLEN: I don't—he's upset.

PEGGY: What?

ELLEN: He's very upset.

PEGGY [*washing her hands*]: I'm sad that both of my children are alone. There's a lot to be said for living with someone for most of your life. [*Suddenly grabbing* ELLEN *by the sleeve*] This was his idea, wasn't it? All of this.

ELLEN: That's not the point—

PEGGY: Tell me what's going on. What is my punishment, Ellen?

ELLEN: It's not a punishment—

PEGGY: Well, that's the tenor—

ELLEN: Let's wait until Warren—

PEGGY: Why, Ellen, why do we have to wait for Warren?

ELLEN: Because—

PEGGY: What?

ELLEN: It's a family thing—

PEGGY: What? A family—

ELLEN: I guess. I—I—I—

PEGGY: A family thing—

ELLEN: Yes. And let go of me. People are going to come in—

PEGGY [*overlapping*]: Please, please.

ELLEN [*struggling to get* PEGGY's *hand off of her*]: Let go.

PEGGY: I won't—

[PEGGY *hits* ELLEN *in the arm*.]

There!

ELLEN: You're like a child—

PEGGY: You're the child—

ELLEN [*never stopping*]:   PEGGY:
—you're like a baby. Is that   You've put me in this situation—
what you want me to think?

ELLEN [*not stopping*]: —is that what you want me and Warren to think?
   That you can't take care of yourself?

PEGGY: Please don't leave here without telling me what's happening.
   Don't humiliate me in public.

ELLEN: We're not—

PEGGY: You are. This isn't a lunch; it's a lynch mob.

ELLEN: Mom—

PEGGY: Are you moving us somewhere?

[*Beat.*]

   Are you moving your dad somewhere?

[*Beat.*]

   Is that it?

[ELLEN *shakes her head yes.*]

   Whaaaat?

ELLEN: Yes.

PEGGY: Whaaaat?

ELLEN: Yes, we are.

[PEGGY *walks to the stall wall and puts her head up against it.*]

PEGGY: You can go.

[ELLEN *leaves. Lights linger a bit on* PEGGY, *who keeps her head on the wall of the bathroom stall. Then the lights cross-fade to the table where* WARREN *sits. He is getting off the phone as* ELLEN *comes up.*]

WARREN: Where's Mom?

ELLEN: I told her.

WARREN: Told her what?

ELLEN: What do you think, Warren? What do you think I told her?

WARREN: Where is she?

ELLEN: In the bathroom.

WARREN: Why did you leave her?

ELLEN: She wanted me to go. I thought it was the least that I could—

WARREN: You shouldn't have told her.

ELLEN: What would—

WARREN: You shouldn't have told her.

ELLEN: She was begging me; she had hold of my sleeve; she actually hit me in the arm. Aaand she's my mother, Warren.

[WARREN *gets up.*]

Where are you going?

WARREN: I'm worried about her—

ELLEN: Leave her alone, Warren.

WARREN: I think—

ELLEN: Sit down.

WARREN: But she—

ELLEN: She'll be out—did you call Patty?

WARREN: Everything is fine—

ELLEN: She'll be out—

WARREN [as he's going toward the bathroom]: I don't trust her.

[WARREN walks to the bathroom and stands outside the door. We see PEGGY inside. WARREN knocks softly.]

[Softly] Mom?

[PEGGY comes out very quickly. She is completely composed. She stands there.]

PEGGY: You think I'm trying to make a getaway?

WARREN [softly]: No.

PEGGY: I don't know if you can understand this, Warren, but we love each other, and I tried to do what he wanted me to do. That's all.

WARREN [still softly]: It sounds more to me like alcohol and anger.

[As PEGGY moves back to the table, BARB comes out with the dessert.]

BARB: Well, I'm just in time.

PEGGY: Mmmmm, that looks so good.

BARB: And three forks.

[WARREN stands up and remains standing until BARB leaves the scene.]

PEGGY: One will do, I think.

BARB: Getting selfish with your sweets?

PEGGY: My kids don't get dessert today!

BARB [*as* WARREN *and* PEGGY *approach the table*]: Well, I'll give them forks—

PEGGY [*sitting down*]: No, no forks.

ELLEN: WARREN:
We're fine—   I'm not having any.

BARB: All right. Here you go.

PEGGY: Thank you.

BARB: Eat all of it now.

PEGGY: Don't worry about that.

[BARB *leaves.* PEGGY *begins to eat her dessert.* WARREN *sits down.*]

WARREN: Did you want to talk about this, Mom?

PEGGY: No. But I do want to finish my dessert.

WARREN: In my secret life, Mom—

PEGGY: Please.

WARREN: —Dad can carry on a conversation—

PEGGY: I'm sorry.

WARREN: —he can answer my questions; he can walk to the car—

PEGGY: That's been awhile—

WARREN [*continuing*]: In my secret life, my parents were not alcoholics who have worried me into old age.

PEGGY [*calmly*]: That's not a secret life, baby boy; it's a fantasy. No talking at the table, please.

[*Very properly,* PEGGY *takes one bite. She sets down her fork. Beat. Then, at once, she pushes* WARREN's *and* ELLEN's *water glasses onto the table. Both* ELLEN *and* WARREN *gasp and jump. They both take their napkins to stop the water.*]

Oh, I'm sorry. I'm sorry. How embarrassing.

[*Standing.*]

I want to go home.

WARREN [*as he tries to clean up*]: OK.

ELLEN [*motioning for service*]: I'll get the car.

BARB [*coming over*]: What happened here?

ELLEN: And bring it around front.

PEGGY: Both my kids are so clumsy—

WARREN: We'll take the check.

BARB: Don't worry about that. I'll get someone over here— [*Yelling*] Jocko!

[ELLEN *exits to the car. During the following sequence,* ELLEN *gets into the car and turns on the Mozart piano sonata. She listens intently.*]

PEGGY: It's a mess, isn't it?

BARB: You don't look good. [*To* WARREN] What have you all been doing over here? Your mother doesn't look good.

PEGGY:	WARREN:
I'm fine.	I think she's OK.

BARB [almost frantic]: You look feverish. Your face is very red. You want to sit in the waiting area? [To WARREN] I'll bring you the check.

WARREN: Thank you.

BARB [as she walks PEGGY over to the foyer]: She does not look good. [To PEGGY] Can you make it?

PEGGY [as BARB is guiding her]: I'm OK. You don't need to help me.

BARB: Let's go sit over here, Peggy.

PEGGY: This hasn't been my day, has it? I'm OK. I'm OK.

BARB: I want to make sure.

PEGGY:	BARB:
That's fine. I'm fine.	Just making sure.

[They move into the foyer. PEGGY sits as BARB sits down beside her.]

BARB: You're all flushed; you're all red. You want an ambulance?

WARREN:	PEGGY:
She doesn't need an ambulance.	You think I need an ambulance?

BARB: She's flushed.

WARREN: She's OK—

PEGGY: Am I flushed?

BARB: You might be having a stroke.

WARREN: Don't say that kind of thing to her—

BARB [overlapping with WARREN]: Can you move everything? [Looking at WARREN] I was a nurse for fifteen years.

PEGGY: I'm moving.

BARB: Mom had a stroke—

PEGGY: Am I having a stroke?

BARB [*persisting*]: WARREN:
And if we hadn't ignored the signs— Don't tell her stuff like that.

PEGGY: BARB:
I hope this isn't a stroke— —maybe she'd been fine.

BARB: I feel guilty to this day.

WARREN: She's upset.

BARB [*directly to* WARREN]: She lost the use of her left side— [*To* PEGGY] And she's left-handed.

PEGGY: Oh. You think this is a stroke?

WARREN: No, Mom—

BARB: I think you're flushed.

PEGGY: But a stroke?

BARB: It's got me worried. What have your children been doing? What have you been doing?

WARREN [*angrily*]: Bring me the check.

BARB: I wouldn't ignore this—

WARREN: Bring me the check!

PEGGY: I have blood in my urine.

BARB [*to* WARREN]: She has got to see a doctor. [*To* PEGGY] You know, I kind of feel like we're a family, you know?

PEGGY [*softly*]: No.

BARB [*very intimately*]: We're kind of a family in a weird way, aren't we?

PEGGY [*softly*]: Oh.

BARB: So I want you to be well, and I want you to be safe, OK?

[BARB *kisses* PEGGY.]

I'll see you next week, all right?

PEGGY [*weakly*]: Tell your mom I'm thinking of her.

BARB: I will. [*To* WARREN] I was a nurse for fifteen years.

WARREN: And now you're a waitress.

BARB [*quietly*]: You roughed up a kid and they tried to get rid of you—

WARREN: You've got me mixed up with someone else—

BARB: No, teach, I don't.

[BARB *exits. Silence.* ELLEN *listens to Mozart in her car.* PEGGY *remains sitting.* WARREN *remains standing.*]

WARREN: Mom—

PEGGY: Sh! I may be having a stroke.

WARREN: You're not having a stroke.

PEGGY: I'm having a stroke!

[*Beat.* ELLEN *drives the car up to the restaurant.*]

There she is.

[WARREN *comes to help* PEGGY.]

I'm OK!

[*They both go and get into the car. Nothing is said.* ELLEN *drives off.*]

You know, I'm not going to let you take him.

WARREN [*loudly*]: He's gone.

PEGGY: ELLEN:
What?   Warren.

WARREN: We had him removed from the house while we ate lunch.

[PEGGY *grips her face, begins to rock back and forth, breathing heavily. This rocking back and forth is not melodramatic but a visceral response that* PEGGY *uses to get away from her pain.*]

ELLEN: Mom.

WARREN: Are you sick?

[PEGGY *rocks and moans.*]

    Should we go to the emergency room?

ELLEN: Are you sick?

PEGGY [*moaning*]: Ohhhhhhhhhhhhhhhhhhhhhhhh.

WARREN: Pull over.

ELLEN: Should I pull over, Mom?

[PEGGY *drops from the waist.* ELLEN *pulls the car over.* PEGGY *slowly sits back up, erect and looking forward.*]

PEGGY: Where is my husband? Where is Jack? Where is your dad?

WARREN [*very softly*]: We can't tell you.

PEGGY: What?

WARREN [*very softly*]: We can't tell you, Mom.

PEGGY [*yelling*]: What?

WARREN: We can't tell you. Not until—not until—not until we know that you won't hurt him. Then you can see him.

PEGGY: And how long is that?

WARREN: What?

PEGGY: Until you know I won't hurt him.

WARREN: That's up to you.

PEGGY: So forever, maybe.

WARREN AND ELLEN: No.

WARREN: But we need to know, we need to know that you won't—

ELLEN: Hurt him.

PEGGY: But I'm right. He's not home.

ELLEN: Patty recommended a place—

PEGGY: Patty again.

ELLEN: He will be well taken care of.

PEGGY: Will he?

ELLEN AND WARREN: Yes.

WARREN: He'll be fine.

PEGGY: Well. And how do you know?

WARREN: I just know that, Mom.

PEGGY: Well. You know a lot.

WARREN: I want Dad to be taken care of.

PEGGY: Did he know?

ELLEN: We made the decision after the call from Patty. When she called us this morning. Patty knew what to do—

PEGGY: Well.

ELLEN: He didn't know.

PEGGY: So maybe he died.

WARREN: He didn't die.

PEGGY: How do you know? Strangers come into the house and take me away? I'd die.

WARREN: Dad isn't that aware.

PEGGY: He's aware. Take me to him. Ellen, take me—

ELLEN: I'll take you home.

[ELLEN *starts the car and they get back on the road. Silence.* PEGGY *composes herself for a bit, looks out the window. She and* WARREN *stare out the window . . . this should last a bit.*]

PEGGY: That little place never did very well, did it?

[*Drive. Then drive some more.*]

   I suppose you heard about Flavel Spangler.

ELLEN [*quietly*]: No.

PEGGY: She got an infection working in the garden, a little infection on her forearm and she died two days later.

ELLEN: I didn't know that.

PEGGY: Well, it happened.

[*Drive.*]

That's how I want to die. I want to get a small infection on my forearm—and have the germs and bile and pus and shit and dirty, dirty blood spread throughout my body and then kill me in forty-eight hours. Just enough time to send everyone into a panic. Just enough time to spew in my coma. [*Mumbling*] Such a pretty day it is.

[*Drive. Then drive some more.*]

[*Loudly*] Warren, I saw Catherine in the supermarket.

[*Beat.*]

Did you hear me?

WARREN: Yes.

PEGGY: She said hello.

[*Drive.*]

To you, I mean. She said hello to you.

[*Drive.*]

Did you hear me?

[*Beat.*]

[*Mumbling*] I guess not.

[*Then very suddenly,* PEGGY *tries to get out of the car, working frantically. The next few lines are loud and frantic.*]

ELLEN: Warren! [*Reaching for* PEGGY *as she drives*] Mom!

WARREN [*pulling back on* PEGGY]:
What are you doing? Stop it!   ELLEN:
                                    Stop it, Mom.

WARREN [*as he holds on to* PEGGY]: Are you going to stop?

PEGGY: That hurts!

WARREN: Then stop!

[*Silence.*]

    Done with the drama?

PEGGY: Yes . . .

[WARREN *is still holding* PEGGY.]

    Yes!

[WARREN *lets go of* PEGGY. *Silence.*]

    You cannot do this. You cannot. I'm going to find out.

[*Beat.*]

    I'm going to find out where he is.

[*Beat.*]

    I might call the police. What would you think of that? Kidnapping.
    I think the authorities might be real interested.

[*Beat.*]

Torture, too! What I've been put through! What your dad has been put through! The gall. The lack of respect.

[*Beat.*]

I am. As soon as I get out of the car, I am going to call the police. I'm going to say my husband is missing. He must have been kidnapped because he could never get himself out of the house. I'll swear out a warrant for your arrest. And then you will be taken off to jail.

[*Beat.*]

I didn't have the strength to kill him. I didn't have it.

[*Beat.*]

I'm not a criminal. Do you think your mother is a criminal? Is that what you think? Ohhh, listen to that. Listen to that silence, Peggy. Your kids think you're a criminal.

[*Beat.*]

I didn't think of it as murder. I thought it seemed right; it seemed right to me, it just seemed like what I was supposed to do. He was in pain. He said he was ready to go. That's what he said. That's what he said.

[*Beat.*]

I wasn't drunk, Warren. Your dad and I drink. Your dad and I drink quite a bit at times but not all the time. And when Patty broke into our house this morning, I wasn't drunk. Look at me now. Am I drunk now? Well, am I?

WARREN: No.

PEGGY: Oh, he speaks.

WARREN: You are lucky, Mom, that Patty called us. She could have called the police.

PEGGY: And the police would do what?

WARREN: What police do when they think someone has tried to kill someone else.

PEGGY: Oh . . . Will I be arrested?

ELLEN AND WARREN: No.

PEGGY: But if Patty says something—

ELLEN AND WARREN: She won't.

PEGGY: But if she were?

WARREN: We will cross that bridge when we come to it.

PEGGY: Oh no. I don't cross bridges anymore.

[Beat.]

Were you arrested, Warren, when you hit that kid?

WARREN:	ELLEN:
I did not hit a kid.	He didn't hit a kid.

PEGGY: Were the police involved?

WARREN: I grabbed him—

PEGGY: You can't go around grabbing people, Warren. I've told you that myself.

WARREN: I was justified.

PEGGY: Aha!

WARREN: The school board dismissed the charges—

PEGGY: But they warned you, Catherine said. Right?

[Beat.]

Right? Is that right?

ELLEN: They warned him and then dismissed the charges.

PEGGY: And there you go. I just hope you apologized to that poor student.

[Silence.]

[Mumbling] The world is a madhouse, a madhouse. [In her regular voice] I don't like Barb. She's too friendly. She takes liberties, I think. Did you see the way she sat right beside me? The way she put her arms around me? And she was talking to you in that secret way.

ELLEN: I thought you loved her.

PEGGY: She's too friendly. Too touchy. I don't like that. Let's go someplace else for lunch next week.

[Beat. ELLEN pulls the car up in front of the house. They all sit for a bit.]

It'll be different, won't it? It'll be different. Ohhh. Oh, my.

WARREN: I was going to stay with you tonight, Mom.

PEGGY: Why? Why would you do that?

WARREN: Because. That's why.

PEGGY: I don't want you to.

WARREN: But I am going to anyway.

[WARREN *places his hand on* PEGGY's *shoulder.* PEGGY *does not react.*]

You know, Mom, I hear you and Dad every night before I go to sleep.

PEGGY [*looking straight ahead*]: And what are we saying?

WARREN: I don't know—I just hear you talking. I just—from the past—conversations. I lie in bed, Mom; I get so worried about things—

PEGGY: Do you?

WARREN: About everything—

PEGGY: You're alone—

WARREN: I keep thinking my heart is dissolving—

PEGGY:	ELLEN [*softly*]:
I don't know what I can do about that.	Warren.

WARREN: I feel like I'm having a heart attack because I lay there in the dark, my heart dissolving in my chest—

PEGGY:	ELLEN [*softly*]:
I don't know what you mean.	Warren. Warren.

WARREN: And I wish my mom and dad could help me.

PEGGY: Well, they can't, baby boy . . . Your problem is that secret life you live, that secret life you were talking about. And all those white lies you tell yourself.

[WARREN *removes his hand.*]

[*As she opens the door to the car and looks out*] This is going to be different.

[PEGGY *looks to the house but is still in the car.*]

What a nice lunch. Who paid?

WARREN: I did.

PEGGY: Well. Thank you.

WARREN: You're welcome.

PEGGY [*suddenly and genuinely concerned*]: Is the schizophrenic still there?

WARREN: No.

PEGGY: I thought she might be hiding behind the door with a knife, ready to stab me in the back. [*Looking toward the house*] He's with you, isn't he, Ellen?

[*Beat.*]

Am I right? I know I'm right. He's been taken to your house.

[*Beat.*]

You know, don't you, that this is going to be the death of me?

[*Silence.*]

No response. [*Suddenly*] I don't love you anymore. Did you hear me?

[*Her feet out of the door,* PEGGY *stays very calm and cool.*]

I don't love either one of you anymore.

[PEGGY *goes in.* ELLEN *and* WARREN *wait. Suddenly* WARREN *bursts out of the car.*]

WARREN: I DON'T LOVE YOU ANYMORE EITHER!

WARREN:
CAN YOU HEAR ME, MOM!!!?
AND I'M NOT SURE I EVER
DID, YOU FUCKING FREAK!!!!
[*To* ELLEN *in a regular voice*] I want
her to hear me! CAN YOU HEAR
ME, MOM? I DON'T LOVE
YOU EITHER!

ELLEN [*getting out of car*]:
Warren! Warren! Get
back in the car! WHAT
IS WRONG WITH YOU?
STOP IT AND GET
BACK IN THE CAR!

[WARREN *gets back into the car. He puts his head in his hands and stays like this.*]

ELLEN [*getting back into the car*]: What is wrong with you?

[*Silence.*]

[*Very quickly*] What is wrong with you? As if things weren't bad enough.

[*Beat.*]

[*Very quickly*] Like a baby. Like a child. A fucking kid.

[*Beat.*]

Jesus Christ.

[*Silence. Finally* ELLEN *looks back at* WARREN.]

You going to be OK?

[*Silence.*]

Warren?

WARREN [*head still in hands*]: NO!

[*Silence.*]

ELLEN [*very softly*]: When I told Mom I was going to Italy despite Richard's death, she asked me not to because she had been reading about the spread of avian flu to people who have a lowered immune system. She was convinced that my immune system was low because I had been so stressed out by Richard's death. What I didn't want to tell her was that the stress was gone and that I was the most relaxed I had been since Richard's diagnosis. I was relaxed enough to finally feel what his life, his illness, and his death meant to me. And ironically, one of the things it meant was that I was less likely to come down with avian flu: death as a kind of vaccine against death. [*Chuckling*] If Mom only knew how our immune systems fell during today's lunch, right? If she only knew how close she and Dad are to pulling us into the great pandemic.

[*Silence.* ELLEN *turns the CD player on. Mozart piano sonata plays.*]

This is the music I'm working on.

[ELLEN *and* WARREN *both listen.*]

It's great, isn't it? Richard loved this piece.

[*Beat.*]

And so do I. She's looking out the window.

[*Beat.*]

Gone.

[WARREN *finally looks up.*]

WARREN: I'm sorry.

ELLEN [*as she turns the music down or off*]: It's OK.

WARREN: It wasn't OK.

[*Beat, as they look out the window.*]

If I go up, do you think she'll let me in?

ELLEN: I'll wait to see.

[WARREN *starts to get out of the car.*]

WARREN: If Dad is awake when you get home—

[*A second thought.*]

If Dad is conscious, tell him . . .

[WARREN *stops.*]

Tell him . . .

[WARREN *stops again.*]

Tell him Warren, his son, says hello.

ELLEN: I'll tell him. [*Looking out her window, then suddenly*] There she is at the window.

[WARREN *looks.*]

Look at that face. Jesus. What is that face?

[*Beat.*]

[*Softly*] She still loves us. See?

WARREN: Sure.

ELLEN: And we did the right thing.

WARREN: Yep.

ELLEN: It was right.

WARREN: OK.

ELLEN: It was. Hey!

WARREN: What?

ELLEN: It was right.

WARREN: Well . . .

[WARREN *opens the car door. Without looking at* ELLEN, *he grabs her hand. It's an awkward moment. He releases her hand quickly and leaves. He gets his bag from the trunk and walks offstage.* ELLEN *sits in the driver's seat and listens to the music. She puts her head in her hands for a moment. She sits back up and looks to the house. She gives a wave. She listens to the music. As she does so, her face relaxes. The music gets louder. She starts the car and drives as the lights fade and "Moon River" overpowers the Mozart.*]

Ellen (Meg Thalken) drives her mother, Peggy (Mary Ann Thebus), and her brother, Warren (Peter Burns), to a local restaurant.

In the foyer of the restaurant, Barb (Jennifer Avery, *seated left*) welcomes Peggy (Thebus) as Warren (Burns) and Ellen (Thalken) wait patiently to be seated.

Barb (Avery) points out the bartender as Peggy (Thebus) gives him a
flirtatious look; her children are not amused.

Peggy (Thebus, *left*) has a tantrum in the ladies' room.

Barb (Avery) gives Peggy (Thebus) an unwanted kiss.

Peggy (Thebus, *seated left*) tries to jump out of the moving car as Warren (Burns) and Ellen (Thalken) hold her down.

Peggy (Thebus) tells her children that she doesn't love them anymore.

Ellen (Thalken) consoles her "little" brother (Burns).